FOREWORD

Dr. Mary Ann Frost has dedicated her life's work to enriching the lives of others by applying and sharing the teachings of Dr. Alfred Adler. Adler himself was a storyteller who often entertained gatherings of people around his piano, explaining his complex ideas through music. He would be pleased to know that Dr. Frost is also gathering people around the universally enjoyed pages of a storybook.

Dr. Frost's new book explains that we each start life with a paper bag. How beautifully basic. Memories of childhood flood me as I visualize my own childhood lunch sack. She has captured me immediately with emotion. Over the next chapters, Dr. Frost explains Adlerian principles, interlacing simple language and memorable metaphors to bring complex constructs to life.

The essential lessons of how to lead your life have the wisdom of the stoics but also the psychological explanations of Alfred Adler's Individual Psychology. These are presented in ways that speak to one's imagination, intellect and ultimately our ability to apply their learning and improve ourselves. Three cheers for another great book in Dr. Frost's bibliotherapy collection.

Alyson Schafer

This book is dedicated to my mother,

Estella Frost, and to Dr. Alfred Adler,

both of whom have encouraged, inspired,

and enriched my life and work.

Your Life is Like a

Paper Bag

WRITTEN BY
Dr. Mary Ann Frost

ILLUSTRATED BY. NILA SM SORIANO

CONTENTS

PROLOGUE
"My difficulties belong to me." Alfred Adler

Life can be frightening, hard, and, at times, overwhelming.

It helps to have an encouraging perspective - a view

on life that guides you in identifying the things you do

not control, in embracing the choices you do get to

make, encouraging you to manage yourself in the face of

challenges, and to just keep moving forward.

Your Life is Like a Paper Bag offers such a perspective.

It provides a simple way for you to understand yourself

and others, how the universe works, and how to find your

place in that universe.

My sincere hope is that these simple words will encourage

you to understand and accept that while you don't control

everything, you control enough to live a meaningful and

joy-filled life. You control enough to contribute and leave the

world a better place than you found it.

Mary Ann Frost

INTRODUCTION

Your life is like a paper bag.

There are only three things in your bag.

First, what the UNIVERSE drops into your bag.

Second, what OTHERS drop into your bag.

Third, what YOU drop into your bag.

PART I

THE UNIVERSE

"The Universe" might be . . .

Divine purpose?

Serendipity?

Fate?

The way the cookie crumbles?

Circumstances?

Wrong place, wrong time?

Right place, right time?

Luck?

Happenstance?

The stars?

Karma?

Only you can decide who or what

The Universe is to you.

Whatever The Universe is to you,

it drops stuff into your Paper Bag.

The Universe

dropped you into your Paper Bag.

So, The Universe decided whether you were dropped

into a castle or a slum, a suburb, or a farmhouse,

into a hut in Africa, or an igloo at the North Pole.

You had no choice in any of this.

The Universe chose your Paper Bag.

The Universe decided who caught you

when it dropped you into your paper bag.

Those were your parents.

Could have been fishermen or farmers or gardeners.

Could have been lawyers or doctors or garbage
collectors.

Could have been black or white or red or
yellow or brown.

Could have been rich or poor, royalty or paupers.

Could have been thieves or salt-of-the-earth
honest folks.

Whoever they were, you had no choice.

The Universe decided who caught you.

The Universe decided whether your

Paper Bag was alone, or whether

siblings' bags were close by.

It decided who dropped first,

who dropped last, and

who was dropped in between.

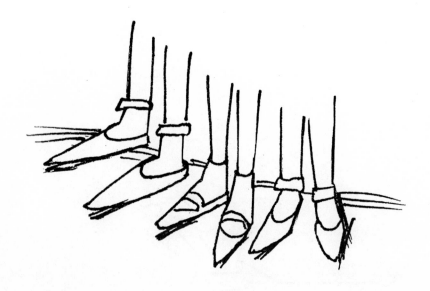

So The Universe decided your birth order.

No choice there!

You got the family that you got.

You got your place in that family.

The Universe did not let you choose how much

time and currency you would find in your bag.

Your hair,

the shape of your body,

the color of your eyes, your height, your smile.

Right down to your fingerprints,

you are unique

- one of a kind -

but you had no say in any of this.

You did not get to choose how you would be smart.

The Universe dropped your unique

INTELLIGENCE style into your bag.

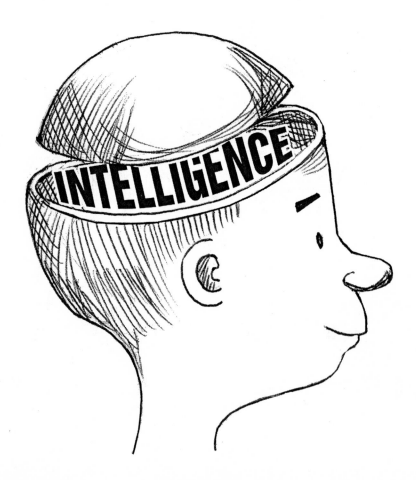

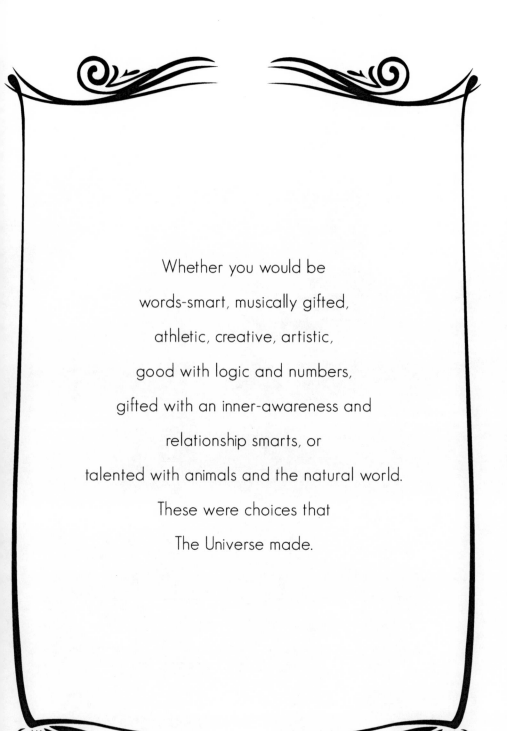

Whether you would be

words-smart, musically gifted,

athletic, creative, artistic,

good with logic and numbers,

gifted with an inner-awareness and

relationship smarts, or

talented with animals and the natural world.

These were choices that

The Universe made.

The Universe dropped your PREFERENCES into your bag.

Do you prefer daily living to be

easy-going and flexible,

or everything in its place and scheduled?

Do you prefer to make decisions

guided by rules or by following your heart?

Do you prefer to work with

data, details and facts or ideas, people and concepts?

Do you recharge your emotional batteries

by going out and meeting new people,

or by staying in with a few close friends

or a good book?

Your PREFERENCES seem natural to you, but you had

no choice. The Universe put them in your bag.

The Universe decided whether Encouragement or Discouragement was dropped into your paper bag.

Maybe The Universe encouraged you by providing early experiences that taught you:

To be **Aware:** balance your needs with the needs of others?

To **Connect:** listen, empathize and cooperate?

To be **Self-disciplined:** to get started, finish tasks, and delay gratification?

To **Contribute:** do your share, no complaints, no avoiding?

To be **Brave:** manage your emotions and make value-directed choices?

If so, The Universe dropped encouragement into your bag.

Or, The Universe might have dropped

DISCOURAGEMENT into your bag:

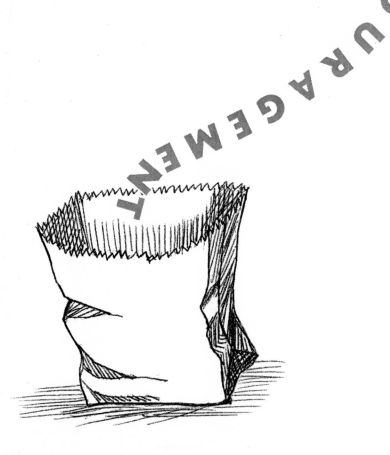

Physical Abuse?

Pampering?

Hunger, poverty, or war?

Discrimination?

Disability?

Criticism or Control?

But here's the thing, even if The Universe did drop

Discouragement into your bag,

you don't need to keep it!

The Universe didn't leave you adrift.

The Universe gave you The Keys To Life:

A GIFT

AN OPPORTUNITY

AN OBLIGATION

These keys will help you steer your course.

Your GIFT is ONE UNIT OF SELF WORTH.

Everyone gets this same amount of self-worth.

Everyone is equally valuable.

Your self-worth is not dependent on accomplishments,

physical attributes, or effort.

It is a GIFT.

All you have to do is accept it gracefully.

Your OPPORTUNITY is

the potential to use your gifts and talents

to create a meaningful, purpose-directed,

and joyful life.

Or not.

The Universe does not choose

what you do with this great opportunity.

Your OBLIGATION is a debt owed to The Universe.
Your chance to say "thank you" for your existence.

You repay that debt by living in a socially
responsible way: balancing the needs of others
with your own and using your unique gifts to leave
The Universe a better place than you found it.

Everyone receives the debt.
Some pay; some don't; some pay it plus interest!

The Universe does not choose
what you will do with your OBLIGATION.

With each passing day,

The Universe continues to drop stuff in your bag!

BIG STUFF

SMALL STUFF

DISCOURAGING STUFF

ENCOURAGING STUFF

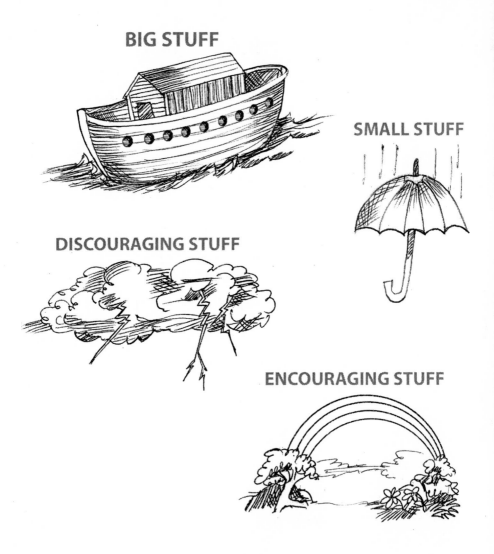

You don't get to decide what stuff

The Universe drops in your bag.

But you do get to choose

how you will respond to it!

PART II

OTHERS

Others put stuff into your bag in two ways:

They can drop it directly into your bag.

Or,

if your bag is parked near other bags,

the messy stuff in Other's bags can leak into yours.

Careful where you park your bag!

Others were dropping and leaking stuff into your bag

long before you were dropped into your bag.

Your biological family dropped DNA

stuff into your bag.

The folks who raised you dropped or leaked

some of their stuff into your bag.

Might have been Encouraging stuff.

Might have been Discouraging stuff.

That's history.

You can't do anything about that stuff!

OTHERS will continue to drop stuff

and

leak stuff into your bag.

By dropping encouraging words and deeds into your bag, others may inspire you toward a lifestyle that is **DREAM-DRIVEN**. Their encouraging words and deeds may motivate you to become and remain empathetic and caring, cooperative, self-reliant, a contributor who is resilient in the face of challenges.

Or,

Dropping discouraging words and deeds into your bag, the Others in your life may nudge you toward a lifestyle that is **DRAMA-DRIVEN**. You may choose to reject your responsibility and embrace behaviors that are self-centered, attention seeking, power struggling, revengeful, or avoidant.

Across your bag's life, Others - spouses, parents, siblings, grandparents, children, caregivers, teachers, mentors, coaches, peers, friends, doctors, pastors, helpers, neighbors, political leaders, co-workers, financial advisors, terrorists, thieves, enemies, advertising agencies, media, and more will - continue to drop and leak stuff into your bag.

Big stuff.

Small stuff.

Dream-driven stuff.

Drama-driven stuff.

You don't get to decide what stuff Others drop in your bag.
But you do get to choose how you respond to it!

You can open your bag wide to encouragement and discouragement. Or, you can close your bag. You can keep what Others drop in, rearrange it to suit yourself, or throw it out.

You don't get to decide whether

Others choose Drama-driven bags motivated by

discouraging actions, thoughts and emotions.

But, you do choose whether you will park your bag

next to theirs.

If you don't like the neighborhood, you can

dream-drive your bag to a better neighborhood.

It is your bag, after all!

Part III

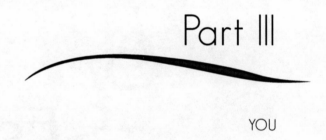

YOU

What do you drop into your bag?

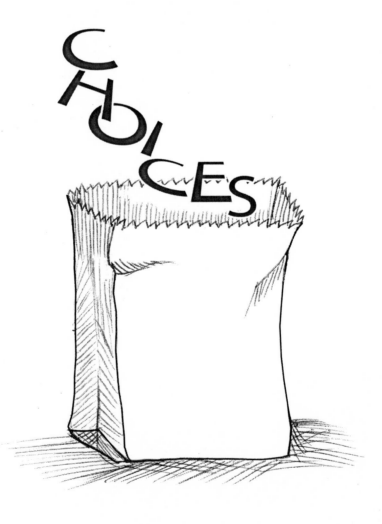

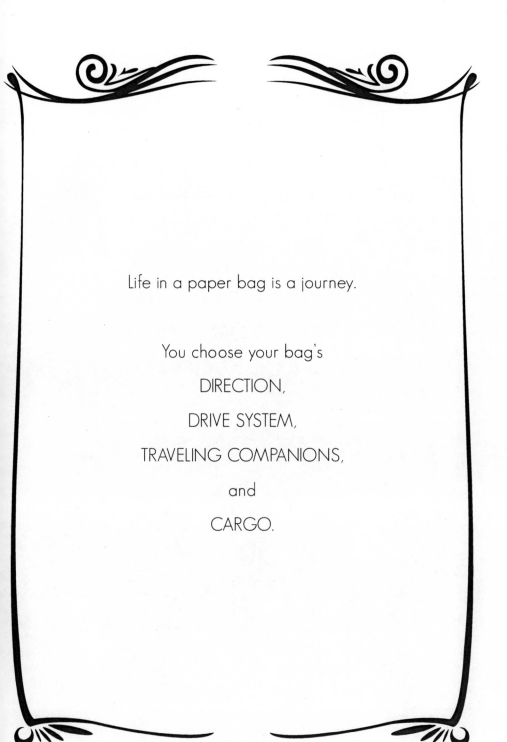

Life in a paper bag is a journey.

You choose your bag's
DIRECTION,
DRIVE SYSTEM,
TRAVELING COMPANIONS,
and
CARGO.

DIRECTION

Your bag's direction is guided by how you choose to

use The Keys to Life that The Universe gave you.

Your responses to

The GIFT
The OPPORTUNITY
The OBLIGATION

provide a GPS for your paper bag.

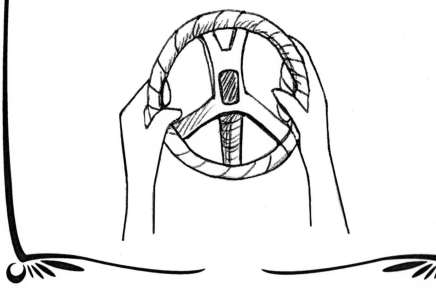

DISCOURAGEMENT

ENCOURAGEMENT

The GIFT As Your GPS

If you want to travel in a discouraging direction,

try dropping criticism or hatred into your bag or

others' bags.

Choose to drop self-loathing in your bag?

Same depressing direction.

Prefer a more encouraging, hopeful direction?

Simple, embrace your self-worth and acknowledge

that everyone else gets the same gift.

Equality is a great GPS!

Equality leads to Encouragement.

The OPPORTUNITY As Your GPS

You choose between crisis and **OPPORTUNITY**.

Want to move toward crisis?
Avoid choices, challenges and the effort of growth.

Prefer to move in a meaningful and joyful direction?
Set goals, be cooperative, overcome your fear of
failure, put in time and effort, and persist on your path.
Your bag's GPS will guide you toward
OPPORTUNITY.

The OBLIGATION As Your GPS

Choose a self-centered direction in life and your paper bag will be mired in the muck of entitlement and dissatisfaction. Your bag will be going nowhere!

Choose to balance the needs of others with your own, and use your unique gifts to leave the Universe a better place, and your paper bag's direction is toward fulfillment, inspiration and meaning.

It's your paper bag.
What direction will you choose?

DRIVE SYSTEMS

Paper bags come with a choice of two drive systems:

Dream-drive and **Drama-drive.**

Dream-drive results in a paper bag energized by values and positive purpose. It fuels staying power and commitment. It attracts hard-working traveling companions who can safely park their bags near yours and inspires Others to choose **Dream-drive.**

Drama-drive is often considered an easier alternative - at least in the short term, but in the long term, it can be an expensive choice! It drains energy and mires your bag down. When you choose **Drama-drive**, it is neither safe nor pleasant for those unfortunate enough to have their paper bags parked near yours.

How do you choose your **Drive-system**?
By investing time and effort in strengthening
your Mental Muscles:

AWARENESS

CONNECT-ABILITY

SELF-DISCIPLINE

CAPABILITY

RESPONSE-ABILTY

The more time and effort you invest in your

Mental Muscles,

the closer you come to **Dream-drive**.

Feeling lazy?

Then, you are in for **Drama-drive**.

To engage: **Dream-drive**, invest time and effort wisely in:

Building **awareness** and balancing your needs and wants with those of others and of the planet moves you toward social responsibility.

Strengthening your **connect-ability** by listening, empathizing, clarifying boundaries, and negotiating differences - moves you toward cooperation.

Developing **self-discipline** by feeding motivation, practicing skills, focusing on priorities, and delaying gratification - moves you toward self-reliance.

Sharpening your **capability** by doing your share of the work well, without reminders, complaint or avoidance – moves you toward contributing.

Managing your **response-ability** by thoughtfully choosing your focus, actions, and thoughts rather than emotionally reacting moves you toward courage and resilience.

To engage **Drama-drive**, all you have to do is invest
your time and effort in:

Self-centered, irresponsible or dangerous pursuits that
deny or ignore the needs of Others and
of The Universe.

Attention-seeking, uncooperative behaviors that
elevate your sense of worth by denying and minimizing
the worth of others.

Power struggling, make-me behaviors, whining about your lack of motivation, and demanding immediate gratification.

Jealous or revengeful behaviors combined with refusing to do your share of the work in life.

Avoiding difficult choices or responsibilities, refusing to consider the consequences of your actions, and complaining about others' behaviors or that life is unfair.

The Universe, and Others, may attempt to influence your choice of a **Drive system**. But ultimately, the choice is yours.

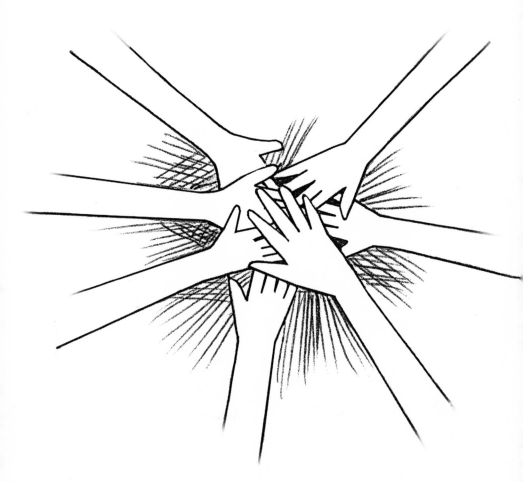

Will you choose?

OR

Will you choose?

TRAVELING COMPANIONS

All around you are the paper bags of
Others – friends, family, community members,
coworkers and more.

Some of the paper bags will be driven by **Dreams**.
These bags will be filled with equality and good will,
time and effort invested in building Mental Muscles,
and an enthusiasm for giving-back
and making a difference.

Other paper bags will be driven by **Drama.** These
bags will be filled with contempt and entitlement,
demands to be pampered, and time and effort
squandered on attention seeking and revenge.

You don't get to choose what others' put in their bags.

But, you do get to choose who parks their bags next

to yours and who journeys forward with you each day.

You get to choose your Traveling Companions.

CARGO

Cargo is all the stuff that you haul around
in your paper bag.

Cargo can be material stuff that you have to
maintain or replace. Cargo might be encouraging skills
that you have built or happy memories.

Your paper bag's cargo might include discouraging
emotional baggage from your family of origin, from
traumatic experiences, or from mistakes that you
made in the past.

Your cargo might be stuff that **OTHERS**
have dumped in your bag across the bag's life.

Or, cargo might be stuff that **THE UNIVERSE** threw in.

What choice do you have?

You get to choose what to do with this cargo:

TOSS IT?

REARRANGE IT?

POLISH IT?

IGNORE IT?

What you do with your cargo is up to you.

But, remember, you don't have to keep cargo if it's not useful, helpful or encouraging.

IT'S YOUR CARGO.

IT'S YOUR BAG.

IT'S YOUR CHOICE.

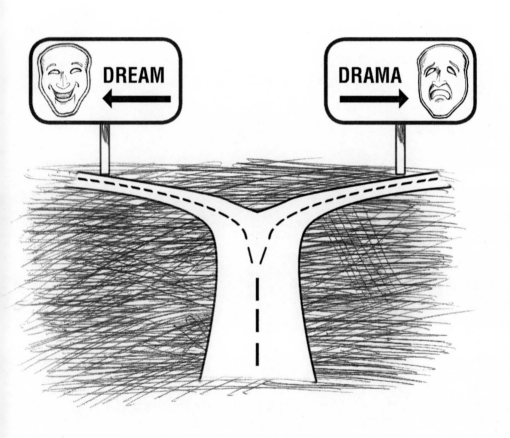

PART IV

FATE

YOU may be confused and believe
that **FATE** is all the stuff that The Universe
drops into your bag.

That's not **FATE**,

that's opportunity or crisis,

dream or drama,

depending on how you choose to see it

and how you choose to act toward it.

Or, you may be equally confused

that **FATE** is the stuff

that Others drop or leak into your bag.

That's not **FATE**.

That's just you choosing or failing to choose

to establish clear boundaries.

If you don't like what Others

are dropping in your paper bag,

CHOOSE to close your paper bag.

CHOOSE to move your paper bag.

It is your paper bag, after all.

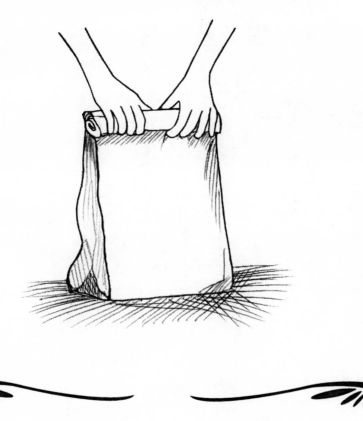

The fact is that the only **FATE**

in your bag is your **F.A.T.E.**

Your: **Focus.**

Actions.

Thoughts.

Emotions.

and what you **CHOOSE** to do with these.

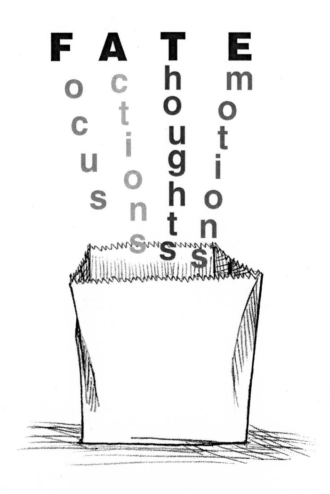

You can choose to change your

Focus, Actions and **Thoughts.**

If you do this long enough, and hard enough,

changing these will change your **Emotions.**

Doing this will take time and effort!

You can choose to invest time and effort in

refocusing on your priorities and

choosing your battles;

acting in ways that keep you in **Dream-Drive**,

motivated by inspiration;

choosing thoughts that encourage you

rather than embracing discouragement.

Your **Emotions** are followers.

They will go wherever your

Focus, Actions, and Thoughts lead the way.

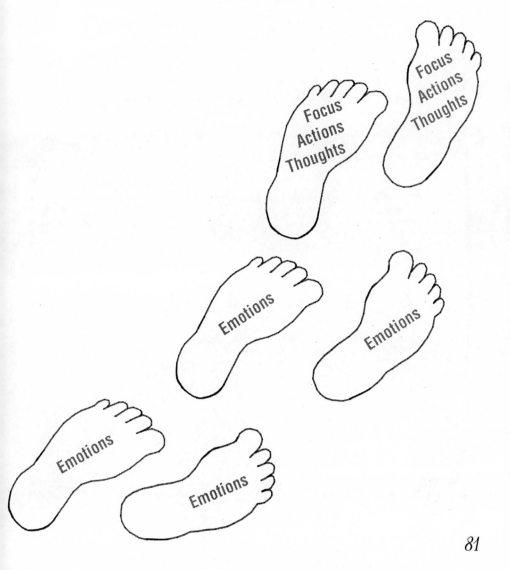

You never did and never will control the stuff that The Universe drops into your paper bag,

You never did and never will control the stuff that Others attempt to put into your paper bag.

These things have nothing to do with

Your **FATE**.

They have everything to do with

Your **CHOICES.**

You choose what to do with the stuff:

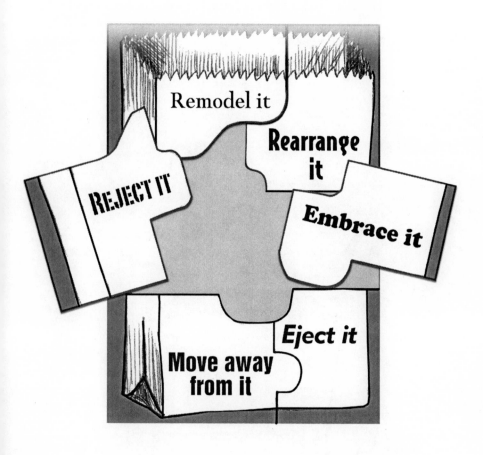

Remodel it

Rearrange it

REJECT IT

Embrace it

Eject it

Move away from it

Your paper bag.
Your choices.

Your **FATE** is not in the bag you were dropped in.

Your **F.A.T.E.** is in the Choices you make each and every day.

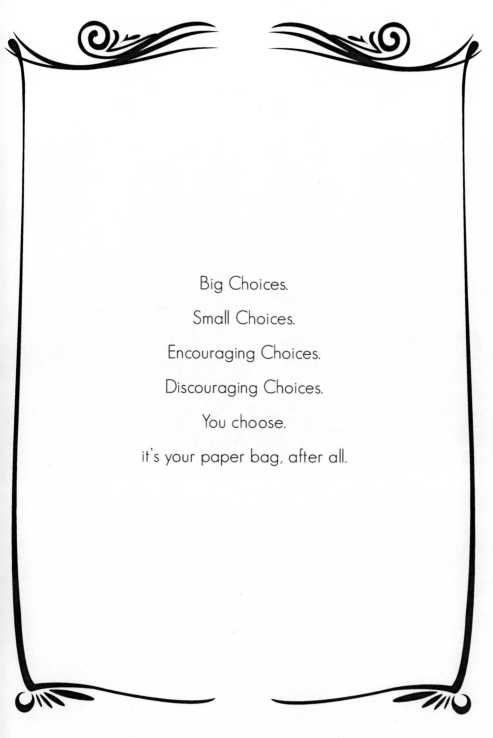

Big Choices.

Small Choices.

Encouraging Choices.

Discouraging Choices.

You choose.

it's your paper bag, after all.

PART V

PAPER BAG LAWS

All bags are guided and limited by universal laws. For your paper bag to be a healthy, encouraging and enjoyable space, you need to understand and embrace these laws.

Bag Law 1: **ALONE**

Space in a paper bag is limited to one unique person - one mind, body and spirit. The sooner you embrace this fact, the sooner you can move on to choosing what to put into your bag, what to toss out of your bag, when to close your bag, and whose bags you want to park near.

Bag Law 2: **UNFAIRNESS**

"THE UNIVERSE" is not fair. You get the bag that you get - no refunds or exchanges. You get the stuff that you find in your bag, nothing more, nothing less. If you don't like any of this, you will need to get over it! After all, The Universe is not fair!

Bag Law 3: **YOUR DRIVE SYSTEM**

Paper bags come with a choice between two drive systems: Dream Drive or Drama Drive.

Dream Drive is fueled by inspiration and perspiration. Drama Drive is fueled by laziness and avoidance. The Universe and Others may influence your bag's drive-system, but ultimately the choice is yours!

Bag Law 4: **OTHERS' DRIVE SYSTEMS**

You never did and never will control Others' Drive Systems. Carrying your bag costs you effort, but results in a bag that is Dream-Driven. Carrying Others' bags or expecting OTHERS to carry your bag always results in a bag that is Drama-Driven. If those around you choose Drama Drive and you get tired of the DRAMA, you can always move your paper bag.

SO,

AT THE END OF THE DAY,

Your life is like a paper bag.

While The Universe and Others drop stuff in your bag,

the most significant contributions come from the choices

you make.

Will you use the Keys to Life as a GPS toward equality,

encouragement and positive accomplishments?

Will you choose to be inspired and motivated by

Dream-drive or demand to be pampered and carried

in Drama-drive?

Will you choose traveling companions with bags full

of hope, enthusiasm, hard work, and dreams, or bags

weighed down by despair and drama.

What will you do with all of the cargo in your bag?

Only you can choose.

After all, it is your paper bag.

ACKNOWLEDGEMENTS

I am deeply grateful to the amazing team who nurtured and guided this book to fruition: Liza Finlay, Nila Soriano and Matthew Lees. I am especially grateful to Matthew Lees who consistently believed in the value of this project and never stopped moving the process forward. I appreciate Alyson Schafer's generosity in taking the time to review this book and write the foreword. Thank you to Wes Wingett who encouraged me to share my writing with others. There are not enough words to describe my gratitude to Richard Mallow for his support, encouragement and daily doses of optimism.

ABOUT THE AUTHOR
DR. MARY ANN FROST

Dr. Mary Ann Frost graduated Summa cum Laude from Purdue University with a B.A. in Psychology; earned an M.A. from Bowling Green State University; and completed a Doctorate in Counseling & Mental Health with a focus on Counseling Psychology and Family Therapy at the University of Toledo. She received family therapy training at the Accademia di Psicoterapia della Famiglia in Rome, Italy. She is Board Certified in Professional Counseling and Relationship Counseling.

She has a private practice in psychotherapy and life coaching which she approaches from an Adlerian perspective. She lives with her family in Palm Harbor, Florida, in a home filled with reminders of the many Powerful Journeys in her life.

ABOUT THE ILLUSTRATOR
NILA SM SORIANO | CESNIL@YAHOO.COM

Nila San Miguel Soriano has been a freelance artist for almost twenty years. She earned her Bachelor in Fine Arts degree at the University of Santo Tomas, Manila, Philippines. In 1984, she immigrated to the US and settled in St. Petersburg, Florida with her husband and three young children. Shortly after, she started a career in graphic arts. While working for different companies as a graphic designer, she started to take on freelance jobs as an illustrator, and soon decided to leave the workforce to become a full-time freelancer.

Over the years, she has developed different illustration styles. She believes that every project is unique and distinct style is necessary to support the intended message of the author.

CPSIA information can be obtained at www.ICGtesting.com
Printed in the USA
LVOW08*2358180614

390482LV00002BA/2/P